Copyright © 2020 Tekkan
Artwork Copyright © 2020

All rights reserved.
First Printing, 2020
ISBN 978-1-7343510-8-8

To contact Tekkan please email:
buddhaboy1289@gmail.com

This book is dedicated to my children, Joshua Kai MacDonald, and Jocelyn Suzuka MacDonald. I am hoping that they will read and enjoy these poems. — Tekkan

How to Read My Poems

I have married the sonnet to the tanka. I tell a story in the sonnet — using three quatrains separated by line spaces, and a final couplet. The story builds to a conclusion in the couplet. The tanka is a commentary, or a counterpoint, to the sonnet — the combined poems have two endings.

I don't rhyme my sonnets, because I want freer expression. I want to be direct in my meaning — I want people to clearly understand my meaning. The metaphors are inspired by Shakespeare, and the (aimed-for) precision is in imitation of Japanese style. Using the sonnet with the tanka, I mix the sensibility of the Occident and the Orient — which I have done by living in England, Japan, and America.

I don't punctuate much in my poetry. I want the words themselves to do the work. There is inherent logic between words, and the forms provide structure. By not using punctuation I hope to direct readers to carefully attend to each word — to appreciate the graininess of words.

Reading my poems silently, say, on a bus, a train, or an airplane, and reading them aloud, may be different experiences. The way I've written, there's not always a pause intended at the end of the line.

Hint: *My poems are to be recited not as lines but as phrases, and a phrase often overflows the break at the end of a line. I pause and take a breath where it seems natural for me to pause. Another person may pause differently than I do.*

Each single poem is a piece of a mosaic, and it is my hope that the collection of poems forms an accurate portrait of consciousness.

My daughter, Jocelyn MacDonald, is a wonderful artist. Her artwork graces this book.

I am Barry MacDonald. I received the *dharma* name *Tekkan*, which means "Iron Man," a settled practitioner of great determination.

— *Tekkan*

Everyday Mind XVI

The milder sunlight
on the verge of autumn
makes the evanescence
of the southward clouds
vivid.

I empathize with the frantic squirrel
In the necessity of the moment
In the middle of vigorous action
And suddenly seized with indecision

When seemingly it's gone too far to turn
Around and yet safety is beyond reach
As it's wavering halfway across the
Street not knowing whether to keep going

Or to go back and it must decide or
Be smooched by the tires of my car while
I understand because it happens to
Me that if I could only calm myself

Before taking action then I wouldn't
Have to rush about like an idiot.

Inattention
and
distraction
lead
to
panic.

I noticed a growth of weeds rising from
The gutters of my house and I retrieved
A ladder for an inspection and found
The wire mesh installed twelve years ago

Was useless for keeping the gutters clear
Of debris and that the gutters on two
Sides of my house were entirely clogged
While the wire mesh was resolutely

Screwed into place so I decided that
The mesh is doing me no good and I
Unscrewed it and reached under it scraping
My arms in the process of clearing the

Debris while swearing at the contractor
Who had bamboozled me twelve years ago.

After a rainstorm
I noticed debris around
the ends of the downspouts
demonstrating that
the gutters are working.

I am getting better at ascending
The arduous hill into Houlton on
My bicycle as I'm able to use
A faster gear and to sprint to the top

And whether I'm facing a headwind or
Being pushed by the wind I'm finding that
Maintaining a steady rapid cadence
Makes the distance go by quickly and these

Mild sunny afternoon rides are fodder
For a peaceful mind as there is enough
Of the sunlight — and not too much — to make
Everything golden and on the decline

Into Stillwater I am hearing a
Chorus of crickets chirping from the grass.

My
ears
and
crickets
are
inspiration.

Kitcat is a mischievous nut case
And he takes the frilly pink sponge that's called
A buf puf from the bathtub in his teeth
And he trots to my bedroom dangling

The sponge by its cord and he drops it in
Front of my door just to mess with me so
This morning I caught him dozing on the
Couch on his back in between sleeping and

Wakefulness and I took his rear paw and
Pulled and pushed it with my hand while humming
A nonsensical tune testing whether
I could keep him suspended between a

Desire for sleep and a feral urge to
Retaliate by lunging and biting.

Kitcat was a little too
drowsy to rouse himself
but he made some
lazy gestures.

I know that plastic flamingoes are not
Examples of especially fine art
And that some people disparage them by
Using the words crass or hideous in

Description of them but I believe such
Valuations are unjust and signal
The traits of superficiality
And impetuousness in the critics

As these people are only capable
Of seeing plastic objects clashing with
Their surroundings but I see delightful
Exquisite elegant magnificent

Flamingoes that are paragons of the
Creative variety of being.

Imagining the
real flamingoes
is a tasteful
exercise.

It is ninety-three million miles away
This morning and I can see it among
The maple leaves outside of my window
As a disk of blazing light and now and

Then an intervening cloud is dimming
Its brilliance and now I can only see
The maple leaves in a boisterous wind
And now I am seeing the clouds clearing

Again revealing radiance as the
Sun is ascending from the horizon
While it's astounding to remember that
Such a normal sight everyone has seen

Is really an illusion as the sun
Isn't rising but the earth is spinning.

The earth is spinning
on its axis
toward the sun at
one thousand miles per hour.

I am well aware that these sunny days
Will not last and I won't be able to
Ride my bicycle in shorts and short sleeves
For very much longer and I really

Do love these afternoons of crickets and
Wildflowers while I'm pumping my legs in
A rapid cadence doing my circuit
Over two bridges around the river

Valley again and again while there's a
Guy I'm seeing quite often walking on
The same trail bare-chested and wearing shorts
And I've passed him at least a dozen times

And every time he's staring at his phone
Oblivious to summer majesty.

Somehow he follows the trail
walking while hypnotized
by the screen of his
smartphone.

I'm seeing monarch butterflies while I
Am repeating my twenty-mile circuit
On my bicycle and I recognize
These are the super generation of

Monarchs that will migrate three thousand miles
From North America to the mountains
In central Mexico to winter in
Temperate weather among what are called

Sacred fir trees and I'm wondering how
Do they understand to make use of
Air currents and how do the different
Groups of migrants every autumn arrive

Repeatedly at the sacred mountains
When they will only make the journey once?

Will these monarchs
I am seeing today
follow currents over
the Grand Canyon and
the Colorado River?

I experience the times of the day
When my energy is diminished and
I also understand that I indulge
Currents of thought that reinforce why my

Circumstances are difficult which leads
Me to wallow in self-pity and I'm
Aware such attitudes are extremely
Unattractive to others because in

Secret most us harbor these gloomy
Sorts of ruminations and when I am
Grumpy it's hard to empathize with you
While I'm expressing quiet aggression

But I also know that the mood will pass
And I will be exuberant again.

Energy and
enthusiasm
reliably
come
together.

It is possible to take pleasure in
The phantasmagoria of the earth
Mixing DNA and protoplasm
That produces a platypus and

Maybe a scientist could offer a
Hypothesis but I am thinking that
He would discount the child like wonderment
That no matter how world-weary I am

Enchantment can be tasted everywhere
And with an impish imagination
I can drop an empty snail shell inside
A tuba a chubby high school freshman

Is sounding in a concert and picture
Curves within curves within resonation.

Do you suppose an
empty snail shell inside
a tuba a chubby boy
is blowing would
rattle?

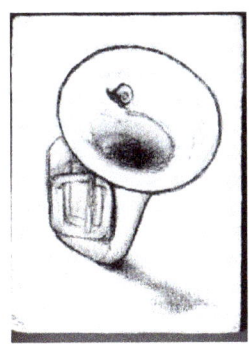

I would think a person would have to be
Crazy to stand on a mountain wearing
A wing suit facing the spectacular
Void of air and distance resolved to jump

Remembering as I do the ancient
Fable of *Icarus* who flew too close
To the sun with the sun melting his wings
Of wax and feathers causing him to fall

While obviously modern nylon is
More reliable than wax and feathers
It would take a lusting for excitement
And a courageous recklessness to leap

Slicing air within the precipices
Enraptured in the ecstasy of flight.

Most of us settle for
a window seat
on an airliner
with peanut snacks.

I take comfort in the contemplation
Of the way that the cosmos works in that
Gravity forms clouds of gases into
The suns and planets and that cyclical

Motion in the form of elliptical
Orbits appears to be a basic form
Of motion right down to the minutest
Quarks that are said to be spinning and I

Take comfort in the speculation that
Time and being and consciousness are not
Linear with a definite and a
Final beginning and end but they are

Just like the setting and the rising sun
Reemerge and life will keep happening.

My quirky
personality
will not
continue
indefinably
but
consciousness
may.

We live within a spectrum of things but
What's really significant are the poles
Of opposites as the world appears to
Be either hot or cold and day or night

And right or left and alive or dead and
Hateful or loving and I can only
Know what summer is in reference to
Winter and can only experience

The wonderful knowledge of compassion
In opposition to indifference
So being also has its opposite
That is nonbeing and one involves the

Fullness of life but the other dissolves
To the absolute emptiness of things.

I cannot
even form
a conception
of the
absolute
absence.

He stopped eating yesterday which was a
Stark difference in his behavior as
He yowls at me incessantly until
I present him with food that compels me

To practice patience because losing my
Temper doesn't quiet him and makes me
Miserable while I appreciate
He's lived since my kids were in grade school and

Now they're grown and living apart from me
And through twenty years Johnnie was a calm
And affectionate cat it's true with quite
A voracious appetite but during

These hard years he's become so bedraggled
Diminishing slowly to skin and bones.

When I found him
lying lifeless
on the basement floor
I knew my home was changed
forever.

In the last years of his life Johnnie taught
Me about patience as he could only
Eat prescription food and he dwindled to
A frail and skinny cat incessantly

Yowling for food which was a burden I
Learned to bear as no matter how much I
Provided he kept on wasting away
And I could usually manage the

Noise and I always felt sympathy but
Occasionally he was way too much
And I found the limits of my patience
Getting angry and yelling at Johnnie

But even then he couldn't be quiet
And I could only keep feeding Johnnie.

I learned to
practice patience
with my
impatience.

When I was growing up I resisted
My Dad's dogmatic and dominating
Personality as he stood apart
From popular culture with vehement

Distaste for rock music and hippies which
Embarrassed my adolescent yearnings
And opposition to him prevented
My appreciation of his passion

For classical music but with hindsight
I perceive that his everyday engagement
With Schubert Mozart and Beethoven on
His cherished grand piano must have been

Among the happiest hours of his
Life when he could escape disharmony.

After all these years
I appreciate him
for demonstrating
how to harmonize.

So much of my childhood was a response
To my father's dominance forming a
Resistance and opposition to him
And of course I didn't understand that

Growing in such a manner only made
Him more dominant as he became the
Impetus of my reaction and in
Cosmic terms perhaps he was the Big Bang

And I've been expanding ever since but
In the interweaving of billions of
People whom I will never meet and of
Billions of events that I didn't cause

Each will have inescapable effects
In forming the nature of who I am.

I hope these poems
will have an
illuminating
and worthy effect
on my kids.

This is a poem about falling down
Which is something that happens to us all
Because we aren't as attentive or as
Graceful as we would like to be and the

Sequence is a slip coincident with
A quirky jerk followed by a moment
Of panic and discombobulation
Leading to the intense awakening

Of impact when all the elements of
Consciousness are concentrated at a
Single point of space and time which may be
Articulated variously from

Person to person but usually
I find myself ejaculating "ow!"

I don't know about you
but the embarrassing
blow to my ego is
worse than the
bruises.

My house where my family lived is not what
It was when it embodied my son and
Daughter and ex-wife and six felines as
Our kids are grown and gone and my former

Spouse is living elsewhere and five of our
Cats whom together we loved have died with
Johnnie departing just this week leading
Me to realize I no longer need to

Close my bedroom door to prevent him from
Entering and yowling before dawn and
Rousting me from my disembodied dreams
And I understand there is no longer

Any occasion within my house for
Me to keep the doors between the rooms closed.

There's no need
between Kitcat and I
to practice privacy.

Seldom can I gaze leisurely at the
Ascending sun without glancing aside
To prevent its blaze from damaging my
Eyes as this morning it appears as a

Mild orange disk without a corona
Similar to the harvest moon and the
Moon is only a harmless jewel of
The sky but this is the mighty sun the

Originator of life on earth shorn
Of its majesty and I realize
Ash in the atmosphere has drifted from
The wildfires in California across

The continent suffusing the air I'm
Breathing and dimming a cloudless morning.

After cooler days
we are having a
resurgence of warmth
but my breathing is
labored with smoke.

The world is always burning as the earth
Has a molten core with pressure building
To bursting with flame and ash and today
California is burning with wildfires

And the air is red with flame while smoke is
Diffusing in the atmosphere crossing
The continent subjecting the country
To a shower of ashy particles

And America is convulsed in a
Political season with a frenzy
Of accusation and dishonesty
Disorienting and dispiriting

Disinformation setting people off
Silently defensively violently.

In the interplay of
air water fire earth
the element of flame
dominates today.

Johnnie is gone now and I do miss him
But his absence is providing a more
Comprehensive understanding of Kit's
Personality and I think I've been

Mistaken by ascribing devious
Motives to Kit's deportment supposing
That he manipulates and bosses
Me about by caterwauling to be

Fed again immediately after
I've just fed him as now I'm recalling
A glimmer of a thought from years ago
That I forgot amidst harassment that

Kitcat has way too much energy and
He is very easily distracted.

Kitcat's not
manipulative
he's flighty.

As the shine of the sun is cresting the
Horizon I can see a mist rising
From the valley and disintegrating
In the crystal air while the prominent

Oak tree and the limbs of other trees in
Pioneer Park are black silhouettes and
Are extensions of the twilight and I
Am grateful to be wearing my winter

Jacket and hat and socks and gloves that are
Counterbalancing the sharp onset of
Cold autumn temperature but as the
Minutes pass the leaves acquire color

With sprinkles of orange red and yellow
And the dew is sparkling upon the grass.

How much longer can
our small gathering of
ex-drunks continue
meeting in Pioneer Park?

There comes a day every year when it's time
To cut and bag the leaves and stalks of the
Hostas and daylilies within my yard
Which I have considered a dreadful chore

But today I am resolved to do it
And my method is much better as I'm
Using a hedge trimmer and not a knife
But whether I suffer through the hours or

Gather enthusiasm will depend
On where my attention goes and today
Is cool and sunny while last year was cold
And wet and I'm not mourning a broken

Relationship as I was last year and
My puzzles today are stimulating.

Cutting and bagging
daylilies and hostas
resembles a ritual
of sowing and reaping
attitudes.

I do delude myself into thinking
That I can turn the necessity of
A repetitive and laborious
Chore into a meditative and an

Uplifting experience but when I
Am doing the actual work I have
To untangle an electric cord and
Strain my legs and buttocks by bending down

To use the hedge trimmer at ground level
And I have to make sure to put down and
Pick up the rake from a place that isn't
Underfoot and when I am attempting

To stuff the stalks and leaves into lawn bags
I have to adroitly open and stuff.

Nothing is more frustrating
Than attempting to stuff
prodigious handfuls
into a halfway-opened
lawn bag.

We ex-drunks reserve a spot on a wall
Where we gather for the display of the
"The Holy Words of Pithy Wisdom" and
First is an admonishment "turn ye off

Ye holy coffee pot" which reminds me
To be awake and another says "let
Go or be dragged" which urges me not to
Be so domineering and a final

Suggestion says "it won't happen like that"
Revealing to me that no matter how
Sure I am about the scenarios
I create in my head when the future

Actually arrives what happens will
Be quite different from what I expect.

Too often
my cogitation
resembles the
planting of
landmines.

I suppose it's a sin to waste space so
The carpenters installed a couple of
Cabinets just below and along the
Ceiling of my house right behind where my

Refrigerator is nestled and the
Cabinets remain empty because I'd
Have to use a stepladder to reach them
But I'm not the only person here and

When I hear a commotion that I am
Not making I assume that Kitcat is
Up to something and this morning there was
A repetitive and mysterious

Knocking which was Kitcat playing with a
Superfluous and unreachable door.

I have a cat within a
cabinet behind the top
of my refrigerator
within the kitchen
of my home.

This is a curious and assertive
Creature possessing eight squiggly limbs
And a bulbous head with clever eyes and
An inventive mind capable of the

Tricks of camouflage and of evasion
As its entire body is squishy
And it can squeeze itself through narrow gaps
To hide within a den that functions as

A sanctuary and it is also
Able to fluidly pounce on its prey
Smothering and biting with a beak and
Imparting venom but an observer

Would have to submerge and swim among the
Kelp forests and coral reefs of the sea.

Oceans naturally
inspire mystery and
people have mythologized
the elusive
octopus.

Oh happy white page you are my trusted
Companion and I can come to you when
I need to communicate and when I
Am bursting with a sudden urgency

To epitomize and articulate
An aspect of my life that I have not
Yet completely digested and I know
The act of engaging with you and of

Expressing the exact words and phrases
That do comport with my genuine and
Heartfelt experience is not something
That I can accomplish all by myself

Because I need another receptive
Entity to draw out my hidden core.

I imagine
many appreciative
faces happily
listening
to me.

Returning home from Hudson yesterday
Rounding a bend and descending a long
Stretch of the highway which I have traveled
Countless times I remembered yesterday

Our returning home from our family
Overland driving vacations rounding
The bend and descending the same stretch of
The road fifty years ago and from the

Back seat of my parents' sedan I could
See a spectacular view of a wide
Expanse of the glittering river but
Today the trees have risen up and the

Welcoming home sight of the river is
Blocked living only as a memory.

The pageantry of the
autumn leaves decade
after decade marks a
deepening expanse
of today.

I am grateful for my new friend who said
To me that I am beautiful because
No one has said that to me before and
She revealed her generosity and

Also the difficulty I have in
Accepting a heartfelt compliment as
Something about the burden of having
An unappeasable ego creates

A craving for approval but when the
Gift is freely given I respond with
A disbelieving hollowness and I
Am grateful for the hours before dawn

When the words that people say to me have
The opportunity to resonate.

I am grateful for
my hollowness where
generosity may
resonate.

The world is like the pulsation of the
Sounding of a temple bell resonant
In crests and troughs and like the vibration
Of the photons of light speeding from the

Sun and also like the orbit of the
Earth around the sun emanating the
Bloom of apple and cherry blossoms in
Spring and the parti-colored leaves in fall

And like the migration of birds in the
Spring and autumn as everything goes and
Comes again in an inexhaustible
Combustible pattern pulsating with

Life as bodies age and pass away and
Other bodies are born and carry on.

I am a drop of
consciousness
alive and one
with an ocean
of consciousness.

In my youth I admired the poets
Who wrote fluidly flowing syllables
Who with a few concisely chosen words
Were able to express the poignancy

And precariousness of living but
As much as I tried sitting at a desk
Ransacking my consciousness for hours
I couldn't assemble a line of words

Because I was stuck on a needle's point
Creating so much unnecessary
Pressure believing with caffeine and with
A tremendous spurt of exertion I

Could compel a masterful moment
Of inspiration and the words would come.

I hadn't learned to
play with words
and to act with
liberated
spontaneity.

I am a drop of consciousness awash
In an ocean of connection often
Making distinctions between myself and
My own circumstances and you and your

Circumstances thinking anyone in
My place should comport themselves as I do
Not realizing that we share the same
Rippling of thoughts and I may respond

More or less with cooperation or
Opposition but we share a pattern
Of possibility creating so
Many personalities not knowing

I couldn't be the person that I am
Unless you are the person that you are.

When I forget
distinctions and
comparisons
I am happier.

While driving home from Minneapolis
Attending to the speeding traffic on
The highway and being careful to be
In the right lanes leading to Stillwater

I kept returning to the sight of the
Harvest Moon sailing beyond the scattered
Shreds of the clouds — and the luminous disk
Possessed me as if it were a fixture

In the night as an ornament to hold
On to in the midst of fleeting chaos
Because I am moving so quickly now
Precariously balanced and wanting

Amidst the velocity and tension
To find the encouraging poise I need.

This morning I strained
my index fingers by
pulling the aging hardware
of double-paned windows
into place.

Solstices and equinoxes go by
Without my noticing because I don't
Follow the calendar so carefully
And I don't have the specialized knowledge

That my friend Jason the ecologist
Does and he can see the uniqueness of
Every season and year after year his
Understanding of nature is growing

While I love apple and cherry blossoms
In spring and parti-colored leaves in fall
Because these seasonal changes apart
From the contention of human drama

Are the embodiment of loveliness
So bright delicate and ephemeral.

Autumn follows spring
spring follows autumn
birth to ripeness
ripeness to birth.

It is a handy trick in politics
To accuse the opponent of lying
When the accusers themselves are lying
And the impact is exponential if

The news people and the politicians
Share a common enemy — and if the
Fodder of accusation rises from
An interweaving of bureaucracy

Composed of distorted and secretly
Guarded information that is proffered
To news reporters regardless of the
Violation of the law then the game

Can be played inexhaustibly because
The bureaucrats remain anonymous.

Distinguishing
what is true
what is a lie
is exhaustingly
tricky.

Jim talked about his regret for having
Smoked for forty years and how he wishes
He'd stopped long before because now parts of
His lungs are useless and sometimes he wakes

From sleep gasping for the next breath in a
Fit of panic yet somehow he makes it
To another day not wanting to see
The doctors because they keep finding things

That are wrong with him and they're really not
Able to help him but the inhaler
Flovent — expensive as it is — does bring
Relief and a truck-driving friend coming

From Mexico brings him the Flovent he
Needs as in Mexico it is dirt cheap.

The five of us
listening to Jim
found nothing
consoling to say.

I do know what gasping for breath is like
Because I've had asthma from childhood and
I recall an incident triggered by
Inhaling the hay dust within a barn

Believing I was going to die but what
Usually happens today is I
Forget to check how many puffs remain
Within my inhalers as the drug is

Draining and suddenly my lungs become
Constricted and for several weeks I
Struggle needing the medicated mist
Of a nebulizer to ease breathing —

I resume with life-giving inhalers
Resolved not to be forgetful again.

The preciousness
of easy breathing
is so easy to
forget.

It happens when I am in a rush and
Not attending carefully that I will
Grab or pull something and crack a nail which
Causes a nagging discomfort when I'm

Putting my fingers in a pocket and
Rubbing the cracked nail against anything
So I'm compelled again to clip and file
My fingernails which I've learned to enjoy

Taking the time as an oasis in
A busy day as I can leisurely
Give my attention to the simple task
Concentrating on creating rounded

Ends becoming a true paragon of
Comely tidiness at least for a while.

I can drum my
fingertips upon
my desk in a
reverie of
joy.

This is a splendid time of the year with
The brightness of the leaves in the mellow
Sunlight giving the days an air of a
Festival and now we are having an

Indian summer with a resurgence
Of warmer temperatures after days
Of frosty weather and I've reopened
My windows and turned the heater off and

Can lollygag about my house upon
The floorboards in the morning in bare feet
Which is a luxury reserved for the
Summer and this afternoon my bike and

I will pedal in the countryside to
Discover whether the swallows have left.

The onset of the cold
compelling a resort
to warmer socks in
the morning brings an
air of seriousness.

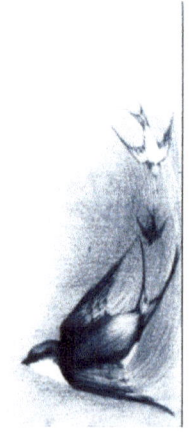

We are far enough along into fall
For the leaves to be accumulating
In the corners of the driveways and by
The curbs of the streets and the yellows and

Reds of the leaves are approaching such deep
Vividness it seems that the leaves themselves
Are radiating light and on a day
Without a cloud the sky is glorious

And contrasting with the silver pendant
Of the moon hanging weirdly within the
Morning sky as the sun is evoking
All the colors of the rainbow spectrum

And a scattering of single leaves are
Circling and wafting down to the ground.

Sun earth and moon
are perpetually
gracefully dancing
with each other.

On occasion I was a grumpy dad
More attentive to the busyness in
My head than to my kids and I recall
My Dad being elsewhere occupied too

Though I witnessed how he dealt with tension
Resurrecting Mozart and Beethoven
On his grand piano for an hour
After lunch every day but I disliked

The piano lessons practicing scales
Remembering only the metronome
Ticking off the time until my freedom
So without much consideration I've

Not imposed my enthusiasms on
My kids believing pressure doesn't work.

I am hoping
in the coming years
my kids will read these words
and remember me
with affection.

My mind is a bowl open to the sky
While I am sitting in Pioneer Park
For a meeting with my friends before dawn
As we are sitting in folding chairs and

Talking about duck hunting and plucking
Feathers and breasting the ducks and I don't
Understand what they mean as I'm alive
To the sounds of traffic emanating

From downtown Stillwater nestled within
Limestone bluffs as the geese are honking and
Flying and squirrels are about and a
Fringe of the clouds is pink from the sun that

Has not cleared the horizon yet but is
Already revealing autumn brilliance.

There is more to notice
than I am capable
of absorbing as the
moment continues
to ripple.

Of all the things to see while the leaves are
At their flowering of autumn color
My gaze is drawn to the silhouette of
My shadow speeding on my bicycle

As if I needed reminding that's me
Propelling myself along not sparing
A moment of ease even as I know
The image is only a symbol of

Who I think I am which is a paltry
Substitute for the kaleidoscopic
Panorama on display today but
By now I know it's better to laugh

At myself to relax and to
Play at racing to a liberation.

In the countryside
I have to be careful
not to smoosh dozens of
woolly bear caterpillars
creeping on the asphalt.

I've been initiated into the
Mystical vibrations of the chakras
And I'm excited to know more about the
Significance of the flowing touchpoints

Of energy manifesting in the
Spine especially because the perky
Woman who has lifted the veil of my
Ignorance is herself an enchantment

And she's discovered that my heart chakra
Is over productive and maybe new
Connections with her the earth and my
Rippling circumstances will dissolve the

Limited scope of my understanding
But now I have more questions than answers.

Does the
undulating
woolly bear caterpillar
have chakras?

The trees are quietly present through the
Years and seldom do they summon my gaze
Except with their vivid colors in fall
And afterward it's a shock to see them

Standing naked and beseeching the sun
With their upwardly reaching bare branches
And then they appear for many long months
Dormant and howling in the winter wind

And they are growing and aging at an
Imperceptible pace and they live and
Die like every living thing but as for
Me I am changing dramatically

Yet if I'm not carefully attending
I don't notice my metamorphosis.

The leaves are brightest
in spring and autumn
demarking incessant
transformation.

Sometimes it's fun to make the letters and
The words that I am sprinkling across an
Untainted page the objects of my love
Reminded as I am of the dropping

And doodling of Jackson Pollock without
Striving overmuch about the meaning
Of the words imagining as I am
That the letters are like the leaves swirling

In the wind with the shape of the letters
Corresponding to the species of the
Trees and with the flurry of syllables
Approximating the gusting of the

Breeze separating the turning leaves from
The trees without a ponderous meaning.

What is the meaning of
winter dormancy and
summer splendor besides
life continues?

This is my 50th poem and I'm
Keeping track on the way to 100
When I may congratulate myself for
Having completed another book as

I am measuring my worthiness by
The number of pages that I've written
Which is becoming like celebrating
The next birthday on the way to frailty

But then I can play with the idea
Of Jackson Pollock dribbling his paint
On an empty canvas and providing
Joy to so many people who are not

Likely to be bothering much about
The meaning of things beyond playfulness.

The weight of
contrived identity
may be dissolved
in playful expression.

I have been writing these poems with the
View that not many people would read them
Beyond a small number of my friends and
Thusly I've felt liberated to write

About risqué topics that I wouldn't
Want my mother to know about and when
She expressed an interest I continued
To feel secure in my secrets because

She's not familiar with poetry and
My poems aren't a page-turning novel
And I assumed she'd never discover
What happened upon page 505

Believing that every preceding page
Is an impeding veil of secrecy.

My presuppositions
are different now
but I'm pretty sure
she won't read this
poem on page
1551.

Before the dawn the valley was dark but
A wide expanse of the water was light
Reflecting an open stretch of the sky
And I was finding the chill in the breeze

Sharp but stimulating and I could see
Several miles downriver the pinpoint lights
Of red and green blinking on the bridge and
On a couple of the boats and slowly

The grainy bark and the remaining leaves
On the trees in the park were becoming
Visible then suddenly the red of
The sugar maple tree was glorious

As the clarity of daylight arrived
And I was happy to be a witness.

It's hard to explain
how exhilarating
it can be to lose
myself in simple
observation.

I've been working with a consultant for
The improvement of my publication
And he's a whiz-bang at conversation
Specializing in gibberish about

His detailed experience conveying
The impression that he's beneficial
But it's impossible to get him to
Focus on what he needs to do for me

As he is urging me to work harder
Even though he knows that I'm exhausted
As I'm sinking into the quicksand of
Reading another of his emails that

Proposes my immersion in a plan
I didn't ask for and isn't helpful.

Scrutinizing a
misbehaving
printing press is
much easier than
fixing people.

I exult within a luxury of
Sanctuary from whatever crazy-
Making agitation is consuming
The hurly-burly activity of

Business by coming to my computer
Letting my hands loiter upon my desk
Centering my chin upon my palm and
Rejoicing with the harmonious joy

Of morning composition selecting
Words transforming experience into
A pursuit for elusive moments of
Insight composing nonsensical lines

Of poetry and reforming trouble
Into a blaze of glittering whimsy.

I can churn and grind
my prevaricating
consultant into
a piquant
tomato paste.

The blades are sharp and ready
The gears and wheels are oiled
I crank the handle
Around and around
And the paste comes spurting out.

A frost arrived along with a forecast
Today for three to five inches of snow
While the yellow leaves are still clinging to
My cottonwood so I'm not able to

Dispose of the leaves before the onslaught
Of winter which for more than 20 years
Has demarcated the pivot of the
Seasons when with the dynamic motion

Of my body I rake and I gather
Handfuls of leaves and stuff them into the
Open lawn bags which is trickiest when
The bag is empty because the bag will

Stubbornly resist staying open and
Many of the leaves refuse to go in.

Little handfuls of leaves
using my left hand to stuff
and my right hand
to hold the bag open
obtains satisfaction.

It's odd to see so many leaves on the
Trees after the first snowfall showing an
Overlapping of seasons with sticky
Snow clinging to the branches of trees with

The dropping of the melting snow and the
Pooling of water within the lower
Places of the landscape and perhaps these
Chickadees hopping in the snow leaving

Tracks and darting their heads about haven't
Seen snow before but I am noticing
A milky overcast sky reminding
Me of uncounted winter days as much

A memory of my body as of
My mind's testimony of endurance.

Having uncollected leaves
scattered about my yard
underneath the snow
is a bothersome
untidiness.

I dreamed about putting on my white snow
Boots again that reach up to just below
My knees and they retain some of their tread
And they are smeared with a grayish grime that

Resulted from my 23 years of
Clearing driveways enduring endless steps
Through crunchy sloshy salty grungy muck
And laces at their tops are serving to

Seal impermeable fabric about
My legs protecting my shin bones from the
Abominable chilling sensation
Of snow sliding all the way down to freeze

The most vulnerable part of me that
Goes stiff before anything else — my toes.

Apparently snow
penetrates my
psychic sanctum
though it doesn't
touch my toes.

They were not like the Honeycrisp apples
That are in the supermarkets and lacked
The crisp tastiness and fresh aroma
Of the highest quality but they were

The last remaining apples from the trees
That I planted in my yard twenty years
Ago and from July I have had the
Satisfaction of eating first the soft

Yellow apples of the one tree and then
The later ripening red apples of
The other but now with snow on the ground
Much earlier than expected I have

Emptied my refrigerator of my
Homegrown fruit and summer is consumed.

I keep forgetting
in the midst of
summer bustle
to pluck the fruit of
my raspberry bushes.

The sight of snow on the roofs of houses
Under a milk-white sky with a winter
Chill in the air that seems to arise from
The snow on the ground is a shock to a

Body even when my mind is busy
With political controversy as
A dampening quietude settles on
The land but this year the transition has

A surprising overlap as a maple
With flaming orange and a cottonwood
With cheerful yellow leaves haven't yet dropped
Their leaves and in my moment of morning

Awakening I am celebrating the
Flux of the symbols of the seasons.

Blue jays and cardinals
sprinkle winter days
with color but maple
and cottonwood leaves
usually don't.

I've gotten a confirmation from one of
My board members about my consultant
And our suspicious are correct — that he
Is having memory problems — and now

We know why he said one thing on Friday
And its opposite on Monday and why
He forgot appointments and belabors
Me with lengthy emails that are devoid

Of substance resolving me not talk
To him for fear that I would erupt with
Words that I would regret and what is to
Do otherwise than to surrender my

Wrath to feel sadness and to give him a
Release from expectations and duties.

A dampening quietude
not of companionship
but of responsibility
is only humane.

My memory resonates when I see
Gulls flying about Stillwater looking
Very much like the seagulls of decades
Ago wheeling in the gray skies about

The long seawall of Galveston Texas
Comporting very well with the ceaseless
Cresting of the waves of Galveston Bay
Where the poignant cries of the seagulls would

Reflect back to me the loneliness of
My self-imposed exile far from my friends
And family when I thought that I could
Find myself by running away but now

The gulls of Stillwater Minnesota
Remind me of youthful exploration.

Sights and sounds
pepper memory
with inspiration
with reverberation.

The sky is white today with a tinge of
Gray imposing an air of somberness
As if we have been overcome by the
Weightiness of winter in the passing

Of days as if someone had stretched a lid
Over the earth as a circumstance that
Cannot be reversed but I can see an
Intense sphere within the whiteness burning

And radiating the whiteness as a
Shining disk almost as painful to see
As looking at the sun in an open
Sky but now the radiance is serving

Only to gauge the height of the clouds and
To provide the clarity of daylight.

I sprinkle letters over
a white computer screen
tinged with gray as if
I were writing a poem
on a winter sky.

The abrupt transition into winter
Is most obviously noticeable
In the sudden starkness of bare branches
With leaves scattered everywhere on the earth

As the leaves are bereft of colorful
Vibrancy becoming dry and drab on
The ground and I am seeing the many
Denuded trees under an overcast sky

With every limb rising up beseeching
The nourishing radiance of a sun
That is withdrawing a measure of its
Potency which is a sobering fact

That there are barren seasons of life and
Perseverance is a necessity.

As winter drags
the novelty of
bare branches fades
and trees become
almost invisible.

A neighbor is burning leaves as I am
Driving by reminding me of childhood
Memories when the burning of leaves was
More often done and I am breathing in

The poignant aroma while the finest
Grains of snow are almost invisibly
Descending from a white sky full of a
Glowing daylight as the height of the sky

Is impossible to gauge as the sky
The light and the descending snow are one
Phenomenon as a crow is perching
On the topmost twig of an oak and I'm

Marveling that the twig can bear the weight
Of a crow who knows what the twig can do.

There is less color
than a week ago
but infinity
abounds.

I'd like to address you my reader with
Appreciation and offer a few
Words of explanation of what I am
Doing exploring this moment at my

Window creating a sanctuary
Of tranquility and allowing the
Sights and sounds that I've been absorbing like
The gulls that reminded me of seagulls

To resonate and I am hoping to
Inspire you to pause over the words
And to recognize the quiet within
Yourself so that the everyday sights that

You've been absorbing like an overcast
Sky may reverberate as metaphors.

This moment of
experience is the
imperishable point
of the spear
of now.

I close the curtains of my house in the
Evening before darkness arrives and when
I rise from sleep I roam about the rooms
Engulfed in the darkness before the dawn

As the nighttime of winter extends its
Wings further into daylight and I take
Comfort in the rushing of the furnace
Blowing warm air throughout my house and I

Enjoy the coziness of walking and
Sitting within the many islands of
The glowing electric light bulbs within
My home as it seems to me that the world

Outside is diminished and the inner
Realm of quiet and thought is magnified.

After all these years
I am more sensitive
and better aligned
with the rhythm
of the seasons.

I may align my energy with the
Sun cresting the horizon and lighting
The bare trees the sides and eaves of the homes
With the wispy clouds drifting south and it's

Easy to be optimistic when day
Is breaking with a vibrant sky and I'm
Here to witness the few moments when the
Angle of the rising sun touches the

Trees with light and then the light diffuses
Leaving the silhouettes of the starkly
Bare trees brown under a transforming sky
As the pace of the clouds is gradual

And the daylight is ordinary but
The clarity of morning is joyful.

Morning clarity
is often followed by
conundrums
nagging details
evening dullness.

I hated having my round boot laces
Come undone as I was pacing about
Stillwater because I'd have to stop and
Stoop over when I'm in a hurry and

When it's cold outside I don't want to take
Off my mittens exposing my fingers
And the ordeal is embarrassing
In the midst of strangers but thankfully

I've been educated about double-
Knotting my laces and it works even
With round boot laces and it's easy to
Take the floppy rabbit ears and twist them

Round again and now I'm liberated
Bounding about unhindered and happy.

The problem with
ignorance is
I'm unaware of it.

I like to read in bed before going
To sleep with my eyelids wavering and
Drowsiness getting the better of me
With an elbow and palm propping up my

Head when the lazy flop of a tail strikes
My face as I didn't notice but here
He is sprawling strategically beside
Me seizing my attention with an act

Of brazen audacity not once but
Repeatedly looping and lashing me
With the tip of his tail flickering as
An explanation point of sassiness

And what could I do otherwise than to
Rouse myself and snatch his face with my hand.

With one hand I seize
his face and let go
with the other I slap
his tummy and Kitcat can't
defend both at once.

If I slept as much as he does I would
Be a pathetic slouching excuse of
A human being and he doesn't do
A useful thing lounging as he does in

A spot of sun or near the duct from the
Furnace where warm air is blowing and he
Gazes at my boisterous busyness
With fluttering eyelids on the verge of

Sleeping but now and then he'll sit upright
Furiously biting a spot of fur on
His tummy or scratching behind his ear
With his rear paw because apparently

He is assailed with itches and I
Think it's great that he is doing something.

But if I attend
too much to him
I find myself
assailed with
itches.

I need to replenish the water in
The aquarium as a portion has
Evaporated and I can hear the
Continuous pouring of the water

Into the tank and reverberating
And I am neglectful when it comes to
Doing things that aren't immediately
Necessary however now I am

Noticing the liquid loveliness of
The pouring of water that resembles
The flowing of a creek over stones in
A secluded wood which is a peaceful

Sensation much better than its absence
Whispering consistently in my ear.

Does the pitter-patter
of poetry approach
the musical quality
of pouring water?

My daughter took wedding vows dressed in a
Kimono in the presence of seven
Of us inside an art gallery by
Addressing her beloved with these words

That she loves his laugh lines and his shaved dots
His warm eyes and his youthful heart and the
Ignorant jokes he makes and even when
She is groaning she loves him as they have

Together painted murals and fled the
Pope kept an animal alive survived
A quarantine moved across the country
From the sands of the Jersey Shore to the

Stone-scattered coast of Lake Superior
Coalescing elements into one.

Together their
days are richer
laughter deeper
hearts lighter.

I arrived at my Mom's house yesterday
To drive her to my daughter's wedding and
As expected she was 15 minutes
Late in getting ready and I soon got

Over that and the ceremony went
Well and I was happy she got to see
Her granddaughter's marriage and this morning
I noticed that the sun visor with the

Mirror on the passenger's side was pulled
Down so apparently during the trip
She took a sneaky peek in the mirror
To check her appearance which is what my

Ex-wife did and also what a girl that
I take to poetry readings does.

Being male
I don't need
a mirror festooned
onto my
sun visor.

When I listened to a recording of
An enlightened master propounding the
Dharma by reciting poetry I
Compared my verses with those that he chose

And concluded that there is too much of
Me in my poetry as the verses
He employed were broad and impersonal
And perfect for his intention and I

Was downhearted but after a while I
Considered I can't be otherwise than
Who I am at the moment poised for
The opening insights that come my way

Enraptured so often by glimpses of
The unexplainable joy in trifles.

Is it not remarkable
that every being
has lived with the same
sun moon clouds
and roses?

Today is unexpectedly warmer
And on the afternoon of Halloween
I am able to ride my bicycle
On the circuit where weeks before the leaves

Were bright to see so much of the color
Is drained away with the corn and soybean
Harvested with stubble stalks and stems where
The wildflowers were and the crickets

Are silent and so much of what was green
Is brown with interspersed piles of snow and
The river is rippling and reflecting
The gray of swiftly moving clouds and yet

The wind is bracing but not icy and
My pedaling is exhilarating.

There is an
austere and lovely
harmony to be
savored.

I keep the stone I found in summer on
My desk absentmindedly turning it
Until its curves are fitting perfectly
Within my palm with my fingers folded

Over it realizing its size and
Shape wouldn't comport with just anyone
As the holding and turning and smelling
Of it is comforting as my mind is

Elsewhere but now I'm wondering how it
Came to be whether it was subjected
To crushing pressure smoothed and rounded by
Eons of flowing water and whether

It was one with the molten rock of the
Lifeless ages billions of years ago.

It's not a homeless
asteroid as the
forces of the earth
are shaping it
today.

I saw it while driving on Halloween
Not knowing the significance of it
And I always appreciate the sight
Of a full luminous moon in the night

Because it reminds me of the ancient
Chinese poets who wrote about the same
Moon a thousand years ago but today
My friends remarked that it was a blue moon

Which doesn't mean as I supposed that the
Moon looks blue but that because it seldom
Happens that a full moon will appear twice
Within a single calendar month so

When the lucky coincidence occurs
We have a catchphrase to celebrate it.

The moon shone in the west
as the sun rose in the east
this morning equally
welcome.

I'm mindful of a message I've received
To love everyone and to tell the truth
Yet the truth is I don't love everyone
And most of every day I give myself

To politics which is about power
And manipulation and people who
Accuse their opponents of committing
The very crimes that they are guilty of

Which creates confusion and bitterness
And endless tribal animosity
And to put even a toe into the
Quicksand of the daily controversy

Is to become immersed in the loathing
And the dread of victorious tyrants.

I know too much about
the rules for radicals
and the manipulation
of mass consciousness
to be complacent.

So today my loving everyone and
Telling the truth will become my *koan*
As today is election day and the
Culmination of a spiteful season

Of politics coinciding with the
Return of warm and beautiful days when
I may take the opportunity to
Rake the fallen cottonwood leaves and to

Stuff them into lawn bags and maybe the
Gathering of the leaves will resemble
The counting of every vote or perhaps
Simple activity will liberate

My melodramatic predicament
And I may relearn to laugh and let go.

You can't really
forget or ignore
or conquer an
authentic
koan.

Because of the early snowfall and the
Chill afterwards I thought that I would miss
My autumn ritual of raking the
Leaves which would spur an awareness of an

Additional chore to be done in spring
Which would nag my consciousness throughout the
Winter even though I would be blameless
But the unexpected reappearance

Of an Indian summer with such mild
Temperatures has cleared the way for me
To take the very simple task in hand
That every year the cottonwood will drop

Its yellow leaves and overcome the ground
And I will summon the will to bag them.

The leaves drop in
different places from
year to year and the
pattern of my thoughts
will vary.

A blue sky in November is without
The blazing brilliance of the summer sun
And when I close my eyes and face the sun
I cannot detect its throbbing presence

But even though the impetus to growth
That raises fruit and vegetables is
Somewhat drained and the quality of the
Light is becoming increasingly bleak

I believe the light of the winter sun
Is precious beyond price as if the sky
Were like a diamond and with a correct
Angle I can see the light refracted

Into all the colors of the rainbow
Because the air and the earth are precious.

A crack in the glass
of a window has revealed
to me the rainbow colors
hiding inside of
winter sunlight.

We have a tradition in November
To turn our clocks an hour backward and
Favor the sunrise over the sunset
And on the morning of the pivot the

Difference was like magic as at once
There was much more of the daylight and
With the shocking reappearance this year
Of Indian summer I was able

To gather and bag my leaves into the
Afternoon wearing a T-shirt and shorts
Which is beyond my experience in
November and it almost seems as if

This is an extraordinary year and
Winter will not come to Minnesota.

I can see the
squirrels
everywhere
frisky in
bare branches.

The pandemic virus has been active
Around the world for perhaps a year and
In America and in Stillwater
We've minimized our contact person to

Person while the presence of the airborne
Virus is forcing people to wear masks
Inside stores and schools and public places
Placing a persisting strain on people

Isolating and exacerbating
The divisions of a nation that was
Volatile before the pandemic and
After the presidential election

Halves of the nation do loathe each other
Portending endless bitterness ahead.

People who are
recovering from
alcoholism and
drug additions are
hard put to be sober.

Half a dozen of my friends and I are
Gathering in Pioneer Park for the
Conversation that our sobriety
Depends on at 7 am resolved

To meet throughout the winter on Monday
And Friday and we are bringing our chairs
A container for a fire and winter
Clothing and this will be an endeavor

To tell our grandchildren meeting in the
Dark before the dawn watching the sunrise
With clarity arising over the
River valley conversing and thereby

Adjusting our attitudes sharing
Openness willingness and honesty.

We look forward to
turning our will and lives
over to a power
greater than ourselves
for strength and guidance.

The oak in Pioneer Park reminds me
Of the distinguishing form of all the
Oaks with its limbs extending in such a
Peculiar and angular beauty and

This morning a large crow is cawing in
The oak sending and receiving cryptic
Messages in the neighborhood until
It flies away as the sun is cresting

The horizon in a sky clear of clouds
And suddenly there are two suns with one
Arising in the rippling waters of
The St. Croix River as I am hearing

The words of my friends in between the sights
And sounds of the park mixing happiness.

Staying sober
growing toward
lighter attitudes
mixes purpose and
unexpected joy.

What is a plinth between friends as I know
Sometimes you tend to go wobbly and to
Droop from one side to another as it
Is tricky to be balanced everyday

So I assure you that I will be here
As your weighty substance bearing you up
Immovable in a topsy-turvy
Environment where beings of beauty

Delicacy ornamentation and
Of ethereal quality need to
Be firmly held and undergirded
So I reassure you I will be here

When the gravity of the earth threatens
To topple you I will become your plinth.

My dear are you one
who doesn't bother with
dictionaries and instead
guesses at the meanings of
words?

No one was to blame when my family
Moved from Hutchinson Kansas to Bayport
Minnesota when I was nine years old
Because my dad got a better job and

I didn't recognize the impact of
Losing my first genuine friend who lived
In the house on the other side of the
Alley longer back than my memory

Can fathom and I don't remember what
We did together after more than five
Decades but there came a day when I did
Realize that the grief of losing my

First friend is alive in me today and
That the way I do friendships was altered.

I trusted Eric
completely and
disappointment
loneliness and
hurt arrived
afterward.

He is almost thirty years old and is
Making his decisions returning to
College to add an accounting degree
To the engineering degree that he

Already has while living in Juneau
Alaska far away from where he had
His childhood growing in surprising ways
Being smart and independent and an

Overnight manager of a deli
Often much too busy to talk to me
On the phone and I'd love to discover
How he arrived to where he is from where

He was but perhaps he himself doesn't
Know beyond the fact that he had to go.

Joshua my son
Jocelyn my daughter
are seizing control
making decisions
navigating the world.

She says when I talk about discordant
Topics or mention a person that I've
Been entangled with that she notices
That I depart from my body meaning

That a passion takes me and I am
Not calmly present but agitated
My breath is labored and shallow which is
A fact that I can verify and her

Words direct me inward asking what I'm
Noticing and often I'm groping for
Answers sensing vibration along my
Spine watching my breath becoming deeper

Longer as she's revealing to me how
Thought and energy are interwoven.

Charkas
instantly
reflect
a shifting
thought.

Temperate and beautiful days are rare
In November so I seized upon the
Opportunity to pedal with and
Against the wind on my bicycle in

My short-sleeved jersey descending into
Stillwater relaxed and cruising as a
Couple of teenagers are cavorting
On my left and one of them launches a

A skateboard directly into my path
Toppling me over the handlebars and
I roll without injury besides the
Blow to my ego and in my shock I

Swear as they apologize profusely
And I discover my bike doesn't work.

My bicycle season is
over as I walk my bike
up the hill to home
as the cold returns
tomorrow.

I was reading the creation myth and
Saga of Middle Earth by Tolkien when
I noticed a yowling commotion and
A cracking in the living room that drove

Me to investigate to observe that
Kitcat had fallen from his perch at the
Open window and he broke an ornate
Porcelain Chinese planter and he was

Agitated and responded to my
Questions by sinking his nails into my
Thigh which I didn't appreciate so
Much but what could I do otherwise than

Evaluate the fractures employ a
Roll of clear tape and repair the damage.

Whatever turmoil Kitcat
digested didn't last long
as he lounged on my bed
before lights out
as usual.

I do meditation before dawn for
The bliss of it and afterward I don't
Easily lose my composure but it
Happens after I've expended two days

Raking and bagging leaves expecting that
The Waste Management guys would come with their
Lumbering truck to toss the bags inside
And be gone with the dratted detritus

Of autumn so when they do not arrive
On the appointed day the gradual
Arising of anxiety with a
Touch of righteous anger tends to take me

Over so I call customer service
And wait on hold expecting an answer.

A pleasant woman
scheduled a courtesy
pick up for today but
now I'm worried whether
they will come.

In Aldi's the inexpensive grocery
Store I'm drawn to the coffee section by
A hypnotizing splash of glossy bags
Of brown orange red and blue reminding

Me of Christmas ornaments and I choose
The light roast ones because they provide the
Most rousing dose of caffeine and their names
Are enticing delicious and tasty

Of Hazelnut of French Vanilla and
Of Morning Brew and the bags aren't very
Big and they don't last much more than a week
But they grace me with the presumptuous air

Of being an unappreciated
Gourmet who finds himself lost at Aldi's.

I open the bag
by pinching and pulling with
thumbs and index fingers
and smell heavenly
Hazelnut aroma.

I settle myself on my cushion in
My living room in the dark with a straight
Back with my legs crossed eager to wash the
Weightiness of preoccupation from

My mind and I start the timer on my
Smartphone and hear the resonant ringing
Of a bell three times and the energy
Begins to flow but then I remember

I forgot to push the button on the
Coffeemaker and smoldering I
Unfold and rise to do the deed before
Resuming the posture and reminding

Myself forgetfulness is a blessing
If I don't worry too much about it.

Percolating bubbling
coffee filling my house
with rippling sound
and aroma is
fetching.

Coffee is a boost on any morning
As welcome and as enlivening as
The sun rising and I can't imagine
Not spooning the non-sugar sweetener

And not pouring coffee into my two
Containers before leaving home holding
Weighty containers while locking the door
Heaving the garage door up and getting

Into my car while handling the coffee
Sometimes relying on the crook of an
Elbow so when arriving at my desk
And window I may summon a glimpse of

Insight and prod my intuition and
Sip a burst of clarity and ponder.

On any morning coffee
is a boost especially
with overcast winter
gloom.

By the time I'm in the bathroom after
Preparing coffee cleaning the litter
Box feeding and watering Kitcat the
Drowsiness of sleep is gone and I am

Washing my face with watery warmth as
The tips of my fingers are splayed about
My face rubbing and splashing with soapy
Enthusiasm knowing as I do

Now is the time for the percolating
Of thought as my stream of consciousness is
Supple and spontaneous as I'm not
Attempting to manage my mind but I

Am letting it go wherever it will
And it's a pleasure just to cogitate.

Drawing the razor
over my cheeks and chin
swiping away shaving cream
from under my nose I am
clarifying life.

I keep the 50-pound dumbbells under
The light table and out of the way for
Convenience after I've exhausted my
Head with poetry and bodily I

Prepare for a shock positioning them
Wide apart as elevated grips for
Pushups or in front of a chair for curls
Resolved to overcome the revulsion

Beforehand exerting utmost effort
Expanding labored breathing heart pounding
Blood pumping the veins about my temples
Throbbing gasping for air near finishing

Counting repetitions but I struggle
And sometimes I am just not accurate.

Apprehension
beforehand
dissipates
into
satisfaction.

The gray of the sky is overbearing
The nakedness of trees is foreboding
Seven inches of snow are forecasted
And winter swallowed Indian summer

But I am not worried about my lawn bags
Because they have been collected and the
Rituals of autumn are now complete
And there's nothing to do but wait for snow

The roads and the sidewalks will be icy
The blizzards will come continuously
The city snowplows will be sweeping piles
Of compacted snow across my driveway

And I will do what I have always done —
Put on my big boots and shovel stoutly.

Seven crows were
stabbing the carcass
of a car-smooshed
rabbit across
the street.

An overcast sky
like the whiteness
of an empty page is
pregnant with
possibility.

—*Tekkan*

www.ingramcontent.com/pod-product-compliance
Lightning Source LLC
Chambersburg PA
CBHW042118100526
44587CB00025B/4100